ON A MISSION

Search and Rescue Team

ON A MISSION

Bomb Squad Technician

Border Security

Dogs on Patrol

FBI Agent

Fighter Pilot

Firefighter

Paramedic

Search and Rescue Team

Secret Service Agent

Special Forces

SWAT Team

Undercover Police Officer

ON A MISSION

Search and Rescue Team

By Tim Newcomb

Mason Crest
450 Parkway Drive, Suite D
Broomall, PA 19008
www.masoncrest.com

Printed and bound in the United States of America.

Series ISBN: 978-1-4222-3391-7
Hardback ISBN: 978-1-4222-3399-3
EBook ISBN: 978-1-4222-8508-4

First printing
1 3 5 7 9 8 6 4 2

Produced by Shoreline Publishing Group LLC
Santa Barbara, California
Editorial Director: James Buckley Jr.
Designer: Bill Madrid
Production: Sandy Gordon
www.shorelinepublishing.com
Cover image: Photoreporter/Shutterstock.

Library of Congress Cataloging-in-Publication Data
Newcomb, Tim, 1978-
        Search and rescue team / by Tim Newcomb.
        pages cm. -- (On a mission!)
        Includes index.
ISBN 978-1-4222-3399-3 (hardback) -- ISBN 978-1-4222-3391-7 (series) -- ISBN 978-1-4222-8508-4 (ebook)
1. Search and rescue operations--United States. 2. Rescue work--United States. I. Title.
U167.5.S32N49 2015
363.34'810973--dc23
                                2015004833

Contents

Emergency! 6

Mission Prep 12

Training Mind and Body 20

Tools and Technology 30

Mission Accomplished! 40

Find Out More... 46

Series Glossary 47

Index/About the Author... 48

Key Icons to Look For

 Words to Understand: These words with their easy-to-understand definitions will increase the reader's understanding of the text, while building vocabulary skills.

 Sidebars: This boxed material within the main text allows readers to build knowledge, gain insights, explore possibilities, and broaden their perspectives by weaving together additional information to provide realistic and holistic perspectives.

 Research Projects: Readers are pointed toward areas of further inquiry connected to each chapter. Suggestions are provided for projects that encourage deeper research and analysis.

 Text-Dependent Questions: These questions send the reader back to the text for more careful attention to the evidence presented here.

 Series Glossary of Key Terms: This back-of-the-book glossary contains terminology used throughout this series. Words found here increase the reader's ability to read and comprehend higher-level books and articles in this field.

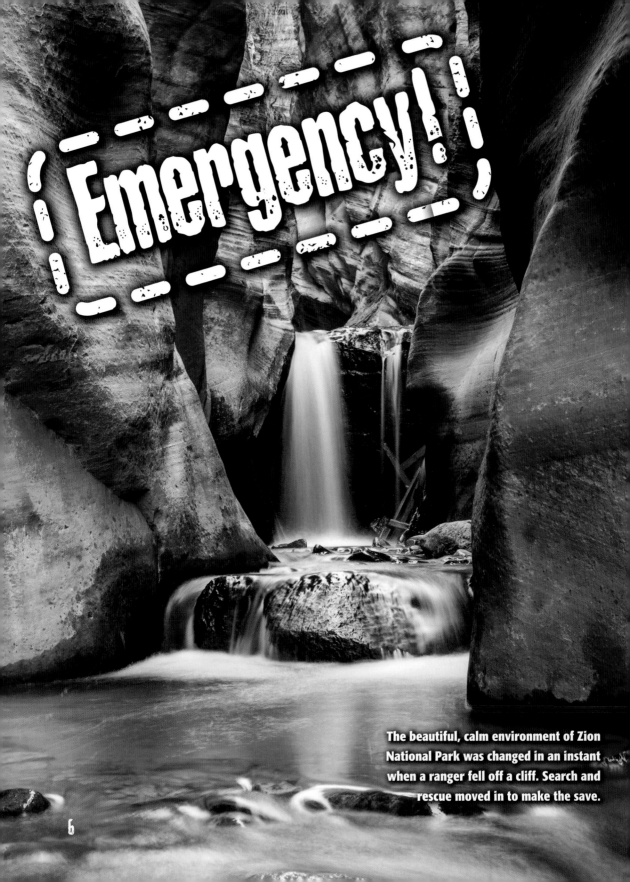

Emergency!

The beautiful, calm environment of Zion National Park was changed in an instant when a ranger fell off a cliff. Search and rescue moved in to make the save.

The beautiful rugged terrain of Zion National Park in Utah, complete with rocky canyons and steep cliffs, attracts tourists from around the world. They are all eager to see the majestic rock formations, sandstone cliffs, and slot canyons that hold centuries of natural history.

They also hold something else: danger!

Every one of those sandstone cliffs has an edge. Canyons have ledges. Rock formations have wildly shaped portions that typical humans can't walk on. Every special feature of Zion National Park has something beautiful to look at and something to avoid falling from.

United States Air Force Captain Marcus Truman, one of the nation's top combat search and rescue officers, still remembers Zion National Park for all those scary reasons.

One of the Zion National Park Rangers does, too.

Truman was training with fellow Air Force search and rescue officers in nearby Las Vegas, Nev. The group was practicing with ropes and **hoists**, as well as using helicopters. The officers were working on

Words to Understand

hoists gear used along with ropes to raise or lower a person or equipment

rappelling the act of using a rope to climb down a steep incline or lower oneself from a hovering helicopter

rappelling from helicopters hovering above the desert at about 100 feet (30 m). The officers used a big, thick rope—about the width of a soda can—to slide down and then jump from when they got near to the ground.

With the ropes, the team members also worked on hoisting each other to different heights. They used radios to communicate with the helicopter and to practice finding their exact positions.

About 150 miles (241 km) away, park rangers trained in search and rescue in Zion National Park were also training. In Zion, the rangers were working with ropes on the cliffs and steep paths.

Sometimes, training doesn't go as planned. It didn't that day in Utah.

A park ranger working in Zion lost her grip on her rope and fell 200 feet (60 m) over a cliff. She was badly hurt. Even if she was capable of getting up on her own, there was no way for her to get out of the steep canyon.

The search and rescue personnel from Zion couldn't find a way to reach her, either. A call to the local sheriff's department provided the same result. While local sheriff's departments all have search and rescue specialists, some have the use of fancy equipment, while others don't always have the technology they need.

Throughout the United States, trained search and rescue personnel have varying sets of special skills. Some know the wooded areas of their hometown inside and out. Others can dive into rivers and oceans, and still others can fly helicopters and airplanes to help locate stranded people. The skills are countless, whether for a small local operation or a huge military effort.

In this case, the call went out to a special unit of U.S. Air Force search and rescue officers. The team that got this call was led by

Search and rescue personnel have special skills to deal with emergencies on land or water.

Captain Marcus Truman. That day in Zion National Park, Truman's group was just a short flight away in Las Vegas, all ready with ropes and hoists on board helicopters.

The seven-person team was assembled. Six parachuting experts were on board with team leader Truman, as the team's pilot flew one of the team's two HH-60 Pave Hawk helicopters toward Zion National Park.

When the team members arrived, they realized they had another problem. The helicopters would not be able to land near where the ranger had fallen. She was stuck in a place too narrow for choppers to go, stranded among the cliffs and the rock formations. The beautiful and famous sandstone cliffs that attracted tourists from around the world were now the one thing this park ranger desperately wanted to do without.

As the helicopter hovered high above, Captain Truman had to figure out a plan. He had to lead his group. He had to search. He had to rescue—and he had to do it quickly. A park ranger's life depended on it.

Later, in the final chapter "Mission Accomplished," find out how Captain Truman and his team came up with the rescue solution. First, find out more about these brave and creative lifesavers.

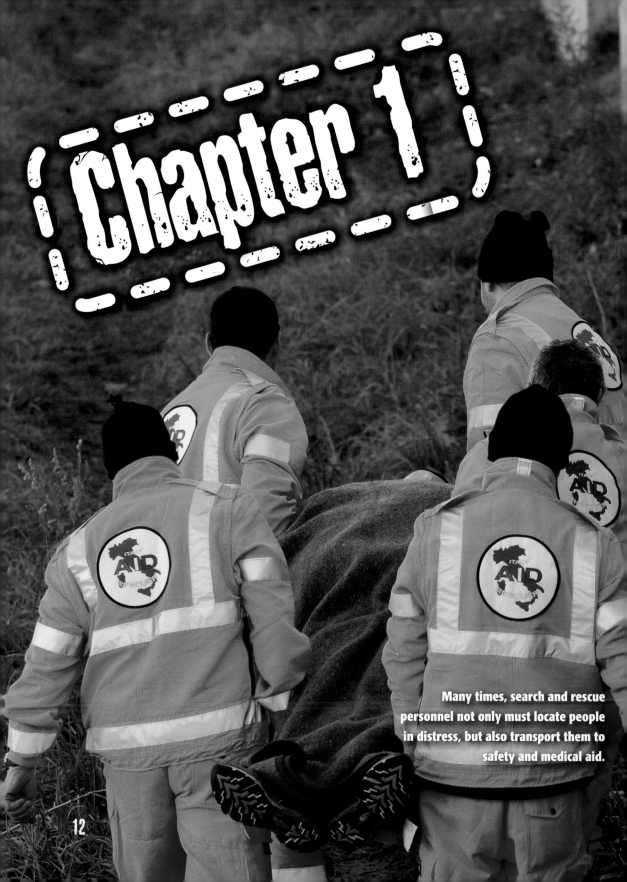

Chapter 1

Many times, search and rescue personnel not only must locate people in distress, but also transport them to safety and medical aid.

Mission Prep

Search and rescue teams save lives every day around the world. They use their intense training, creativity, and courage to go any place a person needs help. For the most part, the job of search and rescue is exactly as it sounds: Search for a lost, hurt, or stranded person, and then rescue them. Sometimes, the difficult part can be in the search. Where was the person last seen? Do they have any technology on them that could give off a signal telling where they are located? What strategies can officers use to find them?

Sometimes the difficult part comes in the rescue—is the person difficult to reach, as was the case with the park ranger stranded in Zion? Just because you know where they are doesn't always make it an easy task to get to them. Sometimes, too, their injuries can make it even harder to get them to safety.

Words to Understand

tenacious having the ability to stick with and finish a task

13

The job of a search and rescue officer covers many different areas. First, and more important than anything else, is a desire to help people. Helping people, though, requires some hard work.

Searching Skills

Search and rescue officers need to know how to navigate the wilderness. If they are on the move in difficult terrain, the last thing anyone needs is for the person searching for the lost to become lost themselves. A person who is already familiar with navigating in places far from "civilization" will have a big jump on becoming a search and rescue expert.

In such remote locations, it might also be necessary to stay longer to continue the search. People in this job don't mind camping out and are expert at making shelters, finding food or water, and creating safe campfires.

They have to be **tenacious**. They can't give up easily. Often their work will take them into danger, and they will put themselves at risk. They need to be able to overcome their fears and get the job done. Search and rescue people are driven and courageous, but are not looking to be stars. They want to save lives and get back to their own.

Along with those personal traits, they may need to know how to jump from planes and helicopters, parachute into oceans, escape wildlife, and even perform emergency medical treatment.

In short, search and rescue officers need to know anything and everything they can about saving someone's life in the toughest of situations.

Volunteers Step Up

Search and rescue missions can start anywhere. Often, they start within a national park or in wilderness areas patrolled by local sheriff's departments. Both areas have teams of experts in search and rescue personnel. National Park rangers must not only know how to protect the wilderness, but they also should enjoy being in the wilderness. Special search and rescue personnel for a sheriff's department can assist law enforcement with this unique job.

Search and Rescue in National Parks

Our nation's national parks provide a stunning variety of natural wonders. Millions of people visit them each year, and some of those people get in trouble in the wilderness. The National Park Service noted that there is an average of about 10 or 11 rescue calls each day in the entire system of more than 400 different areas. The most common place in need of assistance was California's Yosemite National Park. With one quarter of all the calls coming from this popular hiking and backpacking destination, the experts there are kept very busy. Almost half the people were lost or injured during hiking, while boating was the next most common cause for help.

Other search groups are not part of government agencies. On Mount Hood, near Portland, Ore., the Mountain Rescue Association started in 1959 at Timberline Lodge. That makes it the oldest search and rescue association in the country. It now has more than 90 different units across the United States and internationally and is responsible for training rescue personnel on the specific needs of saving lives in the mountains.

One of the largest units that formed as part of this association is the Santa Barbara County Search & Rescue group, an all-volunteer branch of the Santa Barbara County Sheriff's Department. This team covers 2,550 square miles (6,604 square km) of land and focuses on backcountry wilderness for everything from mountain to river rescues. Members go through the same training as agency pros, but are not paid for their work. They are "on call" whenever needed. Many keep their gear in their trucks, ready to race to a rescue scene. Some are experts in fast-water river rescues, while others have training in rock climbing to reach fallen hikers. Just like the volunteer firefighters who work in many small towns, volunteers such as these are vital to their communities.

Whether in Santa Barbara or with other Mountain Rescue Association teams, these experts share a love of saving people. They work as

Rescuers working in the area near Santa Barbara need a wide range of gear to deal with varied terrain.

teams using their skills and knowledge of the outdoors not for money, but as a way to serve.

Extra Help

When the terrain gets too tough, the situation too dangerous, or the mission too difficult, all these volunteer departments and government agencies have a final outlet to call. The U.S. Air Force Rescue Coordination Center can arrange all search and rescue assistance in every state except Alaska and Hawaii, while also providing help to Mexico and Canada.

When a distress call comes in, this center, located at Tyndall Air Force Base in Florida, investigates the request and coordinates with federal, state, and local officials to figure out what type of group is needed. The center chooses the best rescue forces based on availability and need, along with location, terrain, and more. By working with this national agency, local groups can take advantage of the latest satellite technology to track people and search teams. The center can assign teams from the Coast Guard, Air Force, Civil Air Patrol, or other Defense Department groups. By having one national center for this work, communication is made easier, and rescues can happen faster. According to the center, their rescues have saved more than 15,000 people since the center opened in 1974.

Text-Dependent Questions

1. Name the national park that has the most search and rescue calls of any national park in the United States.
2. Where was the first search and rescue association formed, and how much has it grown since then?
3. Name three skills search and rescue officers need to possess in order to properly do their job.

Research Project

Investigate a search and rescue association or department and determine at least three interesting facts about that specific group.

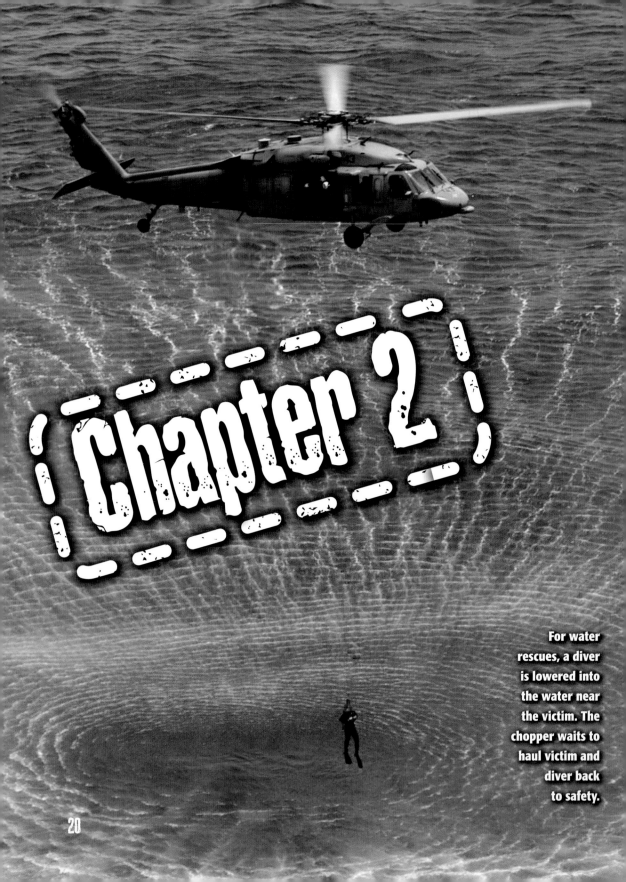

Chapter 2

For water rescues, a diver is lowered into the water near the victim. The chopper waits to haul victim and diver back to safety.

Training Mind and Body

First and foremost, as Captain Marcus Truman tells it, the job of a search and rescue officer is to go out and save lives. "That is our job," he says.

That job starts with training, and training requires sacrifice.

For local sheriff's departments, such as in Santa Barbara County, that can mean one weekend a month dedicated to training. That doesn't even count the number of calls that can come in at any hour of the day or night. While the amount of training required for any group within the Mountain Rescue Association proves immense and difficult, none is more thorough than the Air Force's combat search and rescue team, the top search and rescue unit in the nation.

Words to Understand

classified able to be shared with only a select group of approved individuals

elite among the very best; part of a select group of successful experts

ROTC Reserve Officers' Training Corps: an Army program that trains future officers while they attend college

scenario a specific situation

21

Classwork and Workouts

Everything starts with academic training, Captain Truman says. To even apply for this **elite** group of officers, you must be an Air Force officer, which requires a four-year college degree. From there, you can become an Air Force officer through officer training school, **ROTC** programs, or the Air Force Academy. After all that, the application to join the special Air Force group requires a two-phase process.

Would-be officers must pass a written test and interview, while also getting letters of recommendation from commanders and others. They also undergo intense physical testing. Becoming a search and rescue expert, especially for this special group, demands peak condition.

After the best candidates are picked from the applications, training moves into the second phase. That first week of physical work, says Truman, is the most intense week of any military career. The demanding tasks include running, swimming, marching over rugged land with heavy packs for long periods of time, and survival chal-lenges. Throughout the week, new challenges come at the officers to see how they respond. Making good, quick decisions early in training can show if a person will make the best decisions later on when someone's life is on the line.

During training, candidates have to prove their strength and also learn safe carrying techniques.

During this stressful week, which also includes testing of decision-making abilities, the Air Force starts to form some of the most highly trained search and rescue officers in the nation. Those who pass this first week receive their "ticket to ride the pipeline" of the best search and rescue training. Only about 25 percent of people who enter the week make it out.

Picking a Specialty

Once past the initial stages, search and rescue officers have about a two-year process of learning everything they can about search and rescue. They need to cover every possible **scenario** they could face. Scuba diving? Check. Water survival? Check. Parachute survival? Check. Flight training? Check. High-altitude low-opening jumping? Check. Survival school? Check. The list goes on . . . and all with the goal of helping others.

The first step is a wet one. Trainees learn Air Force combat-dive skills. At the Naval Diving Salvage Training Center in Panama City, Fla., search and rescue officers train on traditional open-circuit scuba diving gear. They also learn how to fend off any potential enemies while underwater. This is more helpful in combat than rescue operations, but it never hurts to be ready.

From there, they move to Pensacola, Florida., to learn how to properly parachute into the ocean. The Army Airborne Parachutist School at Fort Benning in Georgia teaches these officers all they need to know about parachuting from airplanes, whether over water or not. An Army free-fall parachutist course in Arizona and a Navy free-fall

Good communication is a key to safe rescues. This diver is signaling the helicopter above.

course in California round out the parachute training from aircraft. There is more than one way, it turns out, to fall safely from an aircraft.

The training will pay off quickly, says Captain Truman. On one mission in East Africa, he led a team of nine para-rescue men. While much of this life-saving event is **classified**—that is, it's top-secret information he can't share—he did say that the location was difficult for the group to reach. The group hopped onto a French airplane and parachuted into enemy territory. Once on the ground, the rescue group bandaged up injured military personnel and ushered them to a point where they could get safely out of the area and receive proper medical care. Truman says all the training they had allowed them to work together and save nine lives on one mission.

After parachute training, the trainees move down the "pipeline" to more underwater training, emergency medical training, and combat training. Those courses are all taught to many branches of the service at the Survival, Evasion, Resistance, and Escape (SERE) school at Fairchild Air Force Base in Washington State.

Commonly known as survival school, the SERE program is the final portion of an Air Force combat search and rescue officer's training. This type of training was established in the 1950s, but has been updated ever since to improve the ability of the military and others to survive any situation. Truman says that this course covers combat, but also proper survival in a variety of conditions. By throwing wilderness scenarios of all sorts at its attendees, the school can properly train the search and rescue officers to make life-saving decisions no matter the scenario or location.

Following the pipeline of courses, officers enter into a six-month apprentice course. During this time, officers spend more time in the field learning specialized skills. In the end, there are only about 100 combat rescue officers in the world. While search and rescue officers throughout the world undergo serious training to make sure they can save as many lives as possible, quite likely none do it with as much length and intensity as those U.S. Air Force combat search and rescue officers. Still, no matter the training, every search and rescue officer has one job: saving lives.

More Than Just Looking Around

Running a search and rescue operation means much more than simply sending in a team of experts. In many cases, the search is the longest and hardest part of the operation. For this, leaders train in classes that teach them how to "manage an incident." Each time a person is declared missing, a team leader needs to coordinate the work of many people, experts and volunteers alike. Being organized and having a good plan is key. Communicating with the searchers—or setting up communications networks—can speed the process. Leaders also have to learn how to create a search grid on a map, so that all areas can be covered and resources can be put where they are needed.

Classroom work includes learning mapping techniques and how to read satellite imagery. The leaders study how to "read" terrain such as mountains or valleys, how to understand where lost people might go in a location, and how to quickly assess such things as weather, daylight, and the presence of wildlife that all might affect the search.

Finally, after all the physical and technological training, and with knowledge of how to search, the rescue experts are ready to go into the field… and bring people back out safely.

 ## Text-Dependent Questions

1. Name three of the courses search and rescue officers may go through.
2. How do rescuers make sure that an area is well covered during a search?
3. How often does the Santa Barbara County search and rescue group train?

 ## Research Project

Choose either parachuting or scuba diving and explain at least two different styles of that specialty.

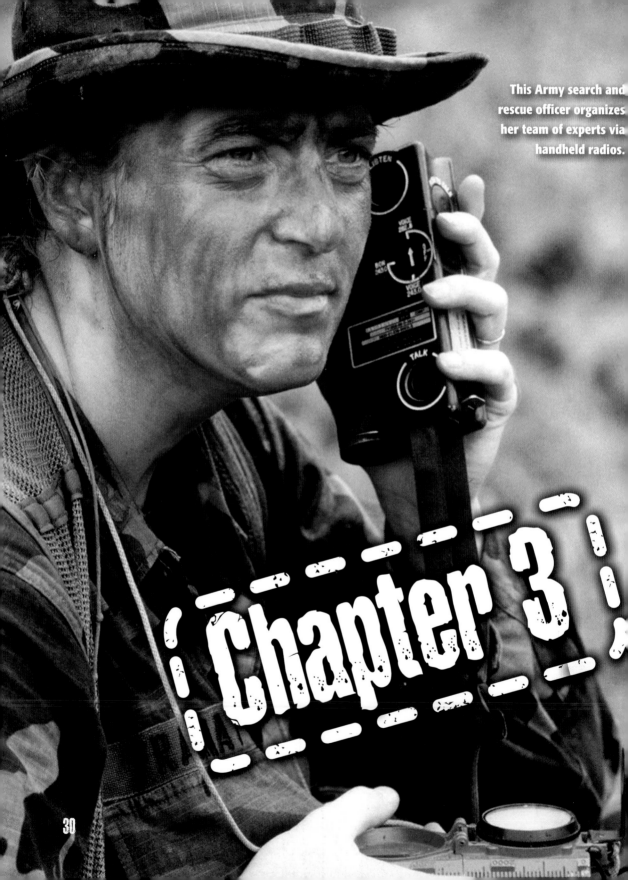

This Army search and rescue officer organizes her team of experts via handheld radios.

Chapter 3

Tools and Technology

While intelligence and bravery are vital to this work, technology also plays an important role. Search and rescue experts use a wide variety of gear to keep themselves safe, to reach their remote destinations, and to make successful rescues. From communications to transportation to emergency care, gear is available to let these experts do their jobs.

Can You Read Me... Over!

The radio is the most important piece of technology involved in search and rescue. Teams use a wide variety of these devices. Each serves a specific function. Some can communicate underwater, a pretty high-tech waterproof way to talk during a search. Some radios can communicate with both the rest of the team on the ground and with the folks in the helicopter overhead. Some, though, can also communicate with the use of satellites, allowing search and rescue personnel to talk to people even

Words to Understand

beacon a signal, usually to a distant viewer or listener

infrared a heat-oriented part of the bandwidth of light invisible to human eyes

navigation the process of finding your way or choosing the right direction to go

stabilized made steady or secure

tourniquets straps or bands around a limb that limit blood flow to a wound on the other side of the world—and, yes, this can all happen by using a radio strapped to a backpack, no matter where in the world they are.

As you may guess with search being the first word in search and rescue, the ability to find people is important. The first phase in finding someone comes with the report—the call that says someone is lost or in danger. The next step is locating that person. While search and rescue officers may have a general idea where the person is, using mapping software can help navigate in the air and on the ground. GPS, global positioning system, can help locate people if they have a device on them that emits a signal. GPS also can help let the rescuers know exactly where they are as well, letting them more easily follow along with their maps.

One of the most useful positioning devices available—used mainly by boats and aircraft—is the Emergency Position Indicating Radio **Beacon**. This beacon can transmit a distress signal to the satellites operated by the National Oceanic and

Atmospheric Administration, which is then relayed back to the national search and rescue system.

Locating Beacons

People heading out on remote trails, high mountains, or the open ocean, can now choose clothing that has beacons or small antennas sewn into the fabric. By wearing this clothing, they can often be found more quickly if they get into trouble. In 2013, for example, 260 people were rescued after using the emergency beacon system.

An additional tool developed by NASA might increase the successful use of beacons. The Distress Alerting Satellite System (DASS) will team with the Air Force's GPS satellites. This new satellite link improves the speed and accuracy of the emergency

PLBs

Personal Locator Beacons (PLBs) are small, handheld devices that can be carried by people in the wilderness or at sea. They can send out a signal in an emergency to help rescuers locate the person. Experts recommend these for hikers, backpackers, and sailors. They also caution that the beacons should only be used in real emergencies . . . and that many are battery-operated, so having extra batteries is a good idea on a long trip. The devices can also be registered so that when a signal is received, rescuers will know who you are and can contact family for assistance or to provide news.

beacon by connecting directly with the Air Force. While still in the development phase, the DASS system is being looked at by international sources, so it would be able to work with a wide range of emergency beacons. The system also has the potential to provide two-way signals. That means a person in distress could get word that help was on the way. Once a person is located, food or medical supplies could be dropped and a rescue team sent in.

Flying Forces

Getting to an injured person quickly is extremely important. Helicopters can reach places an airplane can't. They can maintain the same position for a long time, and can operate in weather that would ground an airplane. For many agencies, the HH-60G Pave Hawk is the rescue workhorse.

This helicopter is specially designed for search and rescue missions. The Pave Hawk can refuel in the air, contains extra fuel tanks, and has an advanced **navigation** system. To make this aircraft even better for search and rescue, night-vision lighting and **infrared** systems can help officers see in low-light searches. Weather radar, foldable blades, and a variety of hoisting equipment make the Pave Hawk the helicopter of choice in the search and rescue world.

Sometimes even a helicopter isn't fast enough, however. The most popular airplane for search and rescue work is the Bombardier C-130. Often the first aircraft on a rescue scene, these airplanes are designed to carry people and equipment. It can also be a great platform for parachuting into a rescue situation, which is often done by military rescue experts.

The Air Force's search and rescue free-fall parachutes include a main and reserve parachute. For the high-altitude low-opening (HALO) type of jumping, jumpers need to have special equipment to keep their body from falling apart in the high altitude. Jumpers will often breathe in pure oxygen before the jump and use special oxygen systems during the jump to ensure they don't run out of oxygen at the high levels, which could cause them to lose consciousness. This is also why the parachutes are designed to open automatically at the correct altitude. To protect from the extreme cold at the high altitudes, the jumpers wear special suits to keep their bodies from freezing. HALO jumps, though, are rare in civilian rescue operations. For those jumps, a standard parachute or paraglide system is used. The rescuer uses handles or ropes to gently steer the chute to a safe landing near the rescue site.

From a helicopter, rescuers can also rappel using ropes. With large packs on their back, they slide down the rope quickly. They use special handholds on the rope to ensure they don't hit the ground too hard. Rescue experts can rappel from 100 feet (30 m) or more in seconds.

Water Rescue Gear

People trapped in water present a special challenge. Often the rescue experts have to move into raging rivers or fast-moving floodwaters to get people to safety. Experts use the term "swiftwater rescue." To do that, they wear protective gear that includes a wetsuit, a helmet, and even padded vests. The teams can stretch rope systems across a river, for example, and

This rescue swimmer has placed the victim in a floating litter, or stretcher, that can be hoisted to a waiting helicopter.

then the rescuer can inch out on that rope to reach the victim. Swiftwater rescue training is an important part of many wilderness rescue organizations. It takes a calm and steady person to plunge into water that could sweep them away at any second.

In some cases, rescuers can use a throwline bag. Using this gear means pitching a weighted line toward a person struggling in the water. If they are able, they can grab the line and be pulled to safety.

When possible, swiftwater rescues are done with boats, usually inflatable craft powered by oars. While some team members move the boat through the current to the victim, others prepare to either grab the victim or enter the water to help. While a whitewater rafting adventure can

Robots to the Rescue

Search and rescue incidents don't always happen in outdoor situations. Sometimes the need for search and rescue comes after a major natural disaster has damaged cities and towns. Earthquakes or mudslides can leave people trapped under or inside fallen buildings. While search experts are the first responders, many now can use robot systems to help find trapped people. Some search and rescue robots can even remove debris as they search. Others are shaped like a snake, so they can more easily maneuver through rubble. As technology continues to improve, expect to see even more robots that can help find people in distress.

sometimes be a fun vacation, in this case, this is not a boat ride anyone really wants to take!

Medical Help

When a person is in distress—often the most challenging aspect of a search and rescue mission—officers use their training to provide immediate medical support and offer any other help needed. They also need gear that is portable, since they might have to lug it for many miles to reach the victim.

Like paramedics, search and rescue experts carry splints and bandages to care for wounds and broken limbs. They have packs that contain a variety of those products so they're ready for whatever they find. The packs might also include **tourniquets**, which can slow heavy bleeding, along with gear to clean a person's wounds before bandaging. They might be able to administer some simple painkillers to the victim, if the rescuers have some medical training.

Along with smaller gear, rescuers can carry collapsible stretchers or baskets they can use to carry people after they've been **stabilized**. These have to be more rugged than everyday stretchers, able to be carried by several people and to withstand some bumps and bangs along the way out of the hard-to-reach rescue site. The rescuers are not a hospital-on-the-move, but they are first responders so they need to be able to handle many medical situations.

Text-Dependent Questions

1. Name one piece of technology you think a search and rescue officer may use that wasn't mentioned in this chapter.
2. What do you think is the most interesting piece of equipment, and why?
3. Why would you use a plane versus a helicopter to get to a person in distress?

Research Project

What new research effort can you find that offers a better way to locate people in distress?

Chapter 4

With both rescuer and victim safely attached, a helicopter slowly raises them up before heading for the hospital.

Mission Accomplished!

Captain Marcus Truman and his team of rescue experts hovered in an HH-60 Pave Hawk helicopter high above the sandstone cliffs of Utah's Zion National Park. Below them, trapped and injured, was a park ranger who had fallen while training with rescue ropes. No one had been able to reach her. The situation was not looking good.

With no place to land the helicopter near the injured ranger, Truman immediately thought of the hoist system by dropping a cable down from the helicopter while the chopper hovered above. However, the helicopter's cable was only 250 feet (76 m) long, not enough to reach the ranger's position.

Truman knew it was up to him to make the right decision...and to do it quickly.

Words to Understand

litter in this case, a stretcher-like basket used to carry injured people out of a rugged area

pelvis the human bone that forms the hips and supports the spine

41

He had the pilot drop the crew nearly three-quarters of a mile (1.2 km) from where the ranger was. "He put us on the ground, and we weren't too excited about separating from the helicopter," Truman says. "It was really rugged terrain."

With such jagged rocks and steep cliffs all around them, the crew members had to build various rope systems, pulleys, and bridges to move toward the injured ranger. As they approached her, the ropes became even more important. The crew had to tie in to the ropes and rock climb on the cliffs to find the ranger's location, using mapping technology all along the route to not get lost.

Once the crew members reached the ranger, they realized that she had multiple bone fractures. Her **pelvis** and leg were fractured. Her skull was cracked. She was starting to have difficulty breathing and was in poor shape. The crew members used their medical training to stabilize her injuries and bandage her up the best they could with the equipment they had carried with them over the sandstone cliffs.

The next step was getting the injured ranger out of the canyon. She was in no shape to walk out—not that walking out was even an option. The search

and rescue officers had built rope bridges and systems simply to get to her. How would they get back out carrying a badly injured person with them?

The officers decided to build a stiff **litter**, almost like a large carrying case. With a rigid bottom and sides, the litter held the injured ranger steady while also giving the team places to hold on.

Truman led the group along each step. He used his radio to inform local authorities of the situation and to talk strategy with the helicopter.

It had taken so much time to reach the ranger that the helicopter was running low on fuel.

Captain Truman exits his rescue helicopter before gathering his team for the hike to where the victim is waiting.

Even though it was the group's only lifeline, Truman sent the helicopter away to fuel up.

Next came the hard part. With the ranger in the litter, the team built even

The best part of any rescue is the ride home after success. The victim is in good hands, and now it's back to the base to wait for another call to action.

more detailed rope systems to slowly move out of the danger area. After an incredible amount of teamwork, the search and rescue officers were able to return to the point where they had started. Still, their work was not finished—this time, they had the injured park ranger with them.

The location was too small and uneven for the helicopter to land. The helicopter hovered low to the ground and Truman's team used the hoist system loaded onto the aircraft to secure the patient and get her safely into the helicopter. Then each team member was hoisted back into the helicopter as well. The next stop was the nearest urgent care hospital.

"The best part about this mission is that the doctor who treated her said that what we had done on the ground when we reached her was life saving," Truman says. "If we hadn't done what we did, she wouldn't have made it."

Saving this injured park ranger was Captain Marcus Truman's first life-saving mission. It certainly wasn't his last. During the team's successful mission in Zion National Park, it called on its training in helicopter rappelling, survival skills, rope work, emergency medicine, and plenty more.

When each call comes in, search and rescue team members never know what part of their training they will need. They might have to climb a mountain, dive into the ocean, parachute into a snow bank, or dig under a collapsed building. They'll take on any challenge because they work toward one goal. As Truman reminds us, a search and rescue officer's goal is simple: saving lives.

Find Out More

Books

David, Jack. *HH-60 Pave Hawk Helicopters (Torque Books: Military Machines)*. Minneapolis: Torque Books, 2008.

Hirsch, Michael. *Pararescue: The Skill and Courage of the Elite 106th Rescue Wing—A True Story of Life, Death and Rescue at Sea*. New York: Avon, 2001.

National Association for Search and Rescue (NASAR). *Fundamentals of Search and Rescue*. Sudbury, Mass. Jones & Bartlett Learning, 2005.

Web Sites

Air Force Rescue Coordination Center
www.1af.acc.af.mil/units/afrcc/

NOAA Search and Rescue Satellite Aided Tracking
www.sarsat.noaa.gov/rcc.html

Santa Barbara County Search & Rescue Team
www.sbcsar.org

Series Glossary of Key Terms

apprehending capturing and arresting someone who has committed a crime

assassinate kill somebody, especially a political figure

assessment the act of gathering information and making a decision about a particular topic

contraband material that is illegal to possess

cryptography another word for writing in code

deployed put to use, usually in a military or law-enforcement operation

dispatcher a person who announces emergencies over police radio and helps organize the efforts of first responders

elite among the very best; part of a select group of successful experts

evacuated moved to a safe location, away from danger

federal related to the government of the United States, as opposed to the government of an individual state or city

forensic having to do with crime scene evidence

instinctive based on natural impulse and done without instruction

interrogate to question a person as part of an official investigation

Kevlar an extra-tough fabric used in bulletproof vests

search-and-rescue the work of finding survivors after a disaster occurs, or the team that does this work

stabilize make steady or secure; also, in medicine, make a person safe to transport

surveillance the act of watching another person or a place, usually from a hidden location

trauma any physical injury to the body, usually involving bleeding

visa travel permit issued by a government to a citizen for a specific trip

warrant official document that allows the police to do something, such as arrest a person

Index

Army Airborne Parachutist School 25

Bombardier C-130 35

Distress Alerting Satellite System (DASS) 33

HALO parachutes 35, 36

helicopter 8, 10, 11, 34, 35

HH60G Pave Hawk 34, 41

Mountain Rescue Association 16, 17, 21

National Oceanic and Atmospheric Administration (NOAA) 18

National Park Service 16

personal locator beacons 33

rescue skills 24, 25

robots 38

Santa Barbara County Search & Rescue 16, 17

satellite tracking 18, 32, 33

Survival, Evasion Resistance, and Escape (SERE) 26, 27

training 22, 23, 24

Truman, Capt. Marcus 10, 11, 21, 22, 26, 28, 41, 43, 45

U.S. Air Force 9, 24, 27, 28, 34, 35

USAF Rescue Coordination Center 18

water rescue gear 35, 36

Zion National Park 7, 8, 9, 41, 45

Photo Credits

Dreamstime.com: Kan1234 6; Jan Kranendonk; Amidala76 12; Roy Pedersen 23; Animalchin 40; Candybar Images 43; Anthony Hathaway 44. Mike Eliason/Santa Barbara County Sheriff's Department: 17; U.S. Air Force/Janelle Patiño: 10; U.S. Navy: Sarah Ard 20; Airman Kristopher Wilson 25; Eric Shuey 37; NASA/Goddard/Rebecca Roth 33.

About the Author

Tim Newcomb is a freelance journalist based in the Pacific Northwest. He writes for *Sports Illustrated* and *Popular Mechanics* about sports design and engineering. His work has also appeared in *Time, Popular Science, Wired, Fast Company, Dwell, Stadia,* and a variety of publications around the world.

Dedicated to my daughters, Adia, Kalanie, and Rilanna, and the pursuit of their own missions!–T.N.